C000225061

THIS BOOK BELONGS TO...

Name: Age:

Favourite player:

2021/2022

My Predictions...   Actual...

The Seagulls' final position:

The Seagulls' top scorer:

Premier League winners:

Premier League top scorer:

FA Cup winners:

EFL Cup winners:

Contributors: Peter Rogers, Luke Nicoli.

A TWOCAN PUBLICATION

©2021. Published by twocan under licence from Brighton & Hove Albion Football Club.

ISBN: 978-1-913362-93-5

£9

CONTENTS

1. ROBERT SANCHEZ

POSITION: Goalkeeper

DOB: 18/11/1997

COUNTRY: Spain

A product of Albion's academy, Sanchez spent time on loan at Forest Green and Rochdale before making his Premier League debut at Tottenham in November 2020.

He soon established himself as the Seagulls' first-choice 'keeper, penning a new contract in February 2021. His excellent form was rewarded with a call-up to the Spain squad for the World Cup qualifiers against Greece, Georgia and Kosovo, likewise Euro 2020.

2. TARIQ LAMPTEY

POSITION: Defender

DOB: 30/09/2000

COUNTRY: England

Signed from Chelsea in January 2020, the right-sided defender has made a big impression since making his Premier League debut against Leicester City that June.

Be it in the full-back or wing-back position, his pace has been a real asset for the Albion when either attacking or defending. An England U21 international, he'll be looking to make further progress after injury curtailed his 2020/21 season.

SQUAD 2021/22

BRIGHTON & HOVE ALBION

3. MARC CUCURELLA

POSITION: Defender

DOB: 22/07/98

COUNTRY: Spain

Marc came through the system with Barcelona and emerged as a regular in the club's B team. After loan spells with Eibar and Getafe, he clinched a permanent move to the 'Azulones', before joining the Seagulls on a five-year contract during the summer of 2021.

With a flourishing reputation, either as a wide player or full-back, Marc was called up to the Spain national squad in the summer of 2021 and made his debut against Lithuania in a friendly in June.

4. ADAM WEBSTER

POSITION: Defender

DOB: 30/09/2000

COUNTRY: England

A player who featured in all three EFL divisions with his first club Portsmouth, Adam gained a reputation as a ball-playing centre-back during his time in the Championship with Ipswich Town and Bristol City.

He joined Albion from the Robins in August 2019 and became one of the first names on Graham Potter's teamsheet. He also gained praise from Pep Guardiola for his performance at Man City last season.

SOLLY MARCH

The side-foot pass is one of the most accurate passing techniques over shorter distances. The ability to find one of your teammates with a pass, even when under severe pressure, and retain possession of the ball is an essential factor in the way the game is played today.

SIDE-FOOT PASS

SOCCER SKILLS

EXERCISE ONE

Set up a 10 x 10m grid. In one corner there are two players and on each of the other three corners there is one player.

Player A starts with the ball. Each player must pass the ball round the square in sequence then follow their pass. A passes to B then runs after his pass and takes up B's starting position. B passes to C and follows his pass to take C's position, and so on. All of the players must control the ball then pass it with the inside of their foot.

Key Factors

1. Non-kicking foot alongside the ball.
2. Pass with the inside of the foot.
3. Strike through the middle of the ball.
4. Keep your eyes on the ball and your head steady.

EXERCISE TWO

The set up is the same as exercise one.

In this exercise the players pass the ball in sequence, A through to D, but do not follow their pass, remaining stationary.

As soon as A plays the first pass, E sets off racing around the outside of the starting point. The players must pass the ball as quickly and accurately as possible while under pressure from E, who cannot tackle but is effectively racing the ball round the square.

The same key factors apply in this exercise as in the first, but the players are required to be able to pass the ball accurately while under pressure.

Any team who can retain possession through good accurate passing will always make it very difficult for the opposition. The side-foot pass is one of the most accurate passing techniques.

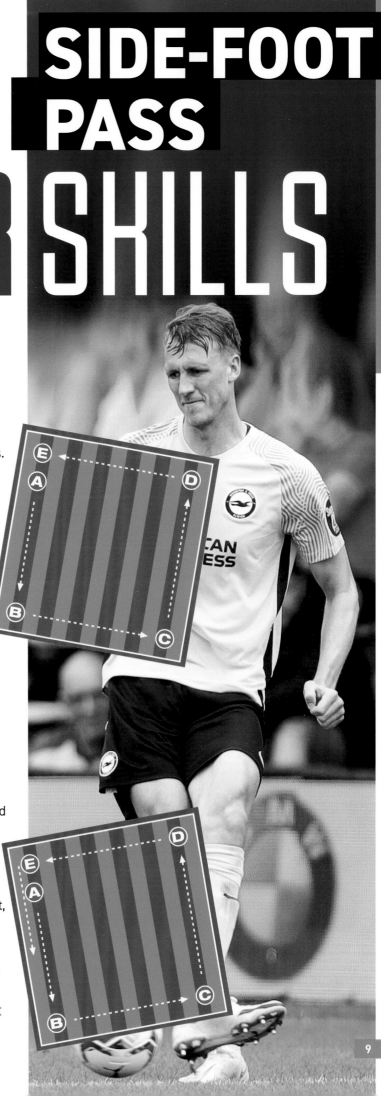

GRAHAM MOSELEY

Goalkeeper Graham Moseley joined Brighton from Derby County in 1977 and established himself as the club's first choice 'keeper during a highly successful period of Albion's history.

He kept nine clean sheets in the Seagulls' 1978/79 promotion-winning campaign as top-flight football came to Sussex for the first time. His heroics between the sticks were a vital factor in Albion maintaining First Division status from 1979 to 1983.

Moseley was also in inspired form as Brighton were FA Cup finalists in 1983. Injuries hampered his final seasons with the club but be was voted Player of the Season in 1984/85 and after 224 games for the club he joined Cardiff City in 1986.

SEAGULLS HEROES

VOICE

Charged with organising the defensive unit in front of him, goalkeeper Moseley would often be heard barking instructions to his teammates. With the whole pitch in his sight it is an important part of the goalkeeper's role to advise teammates of the dangers he can spot.

FEET

Graham Moseley kept goal for Albion long before the back-pass rule was introduced, however he still used his feet to great effect. His kicking could be relied upon to clear danger swiftly upfield and he would often sprint off his line to thwart attackers in a one-on-one situation.

EYES

Always keeping a close eye on the ball, Graham used his sight to judge the flight of crosses and the speed of shots heading his way. Sight is such a vital part of goalkeeping, particularly when quickly assessing whether to come for a ball or leave it for a defender.

HANDS

Blessed with the ability to quickly bring his hands into action to repel the opposition's efforts on goal, Mosley could always be relied upon to pull off saves and use his hands effectively to either gather the ball or push it to safety.

```
A G F G O L D E N G O A L A A V
O C L E A N S H E E T N T X O A
D R I B B L I N G A Y H B L U C
E B P H R N R U T F F Y U R C V
A F F H I T T H E W O O D W O R K M C G
D I L C E N S X D T V R C G R G E O T S
B M A D J P Z E U I W J F N E A D E Z M
A R P K U L I E F S B M A M P I K O S R
L Q A T A T M S D O E M T R P J P Q P A
L Y V C P O A G O I D U A A I Y T N B I
S I W U E T G T A R N V B T K A H V W N
P R C L I N I C A L F I N I S H E R N B
E R Z N S T C H X M A M A M I E N L A O
C Q E H C N S H Y O S U J G L T U E M W
I O A F O S P T E W R O D B Z A M X T K
A J I N F F O X I N T H E B O X B F E I
L K A D E A N T Y V N R K B S Q I C G C
I M G F M U G I A N T K I L L I N G R K
S X P B U H E L G L O R T N O C L L A B
T H E B E A U T I F U L G A M E S P T T
```

SOCCER SEARCH

Ball Control	Clinical Finisher	Flip Flap	Hard Man	Rainbow Kick
Bicycle Kick	Cruyff Turn	Fox in the Box	Hit the Woodwork	Skipper
Boot it	Cup-tied	Gaffer	Magic Sponge	Target Man
Brace	Dead-ball Specialist	Giant-killing	Man On	The Beautiful Game
Clean Sheet	Dribbling	Golden Goal	Nutmeg	Treble

ANSWERS ON PAGE 62

11

SQUAD 2021/22

5. LEWIS DUNK

POSITION: Defender

DOB: 21/11/1991

COUNTRY: England

The club captain again led by example in 2020/21 and was rewarded with another Players' Player of the Season award.

A commanding presence at centre-half, 'Dunky' has made over 300 league appearances for the Seagulls since making his debut at MK Dons in May 2010. He has just one England cap to his name, despite a consistently high level of performance in the Premier League.

7. AARON CONNOLLY

POSITION: Forward

DOB: 28/1/2000

COUNTRY: Republic of Ireland

Joining Albion's academy in 2016, Aaron was prolific in the junior ranks - earning a first-team debut against Barnet in the EFL Cup in August 2017.

His breakthrough season came in 2019/20 when he netted a memorable brace against Tottenham in October 2019. He made his Republic of Ireland debut a few days later against Georgia and has remained a squad regular for club and country.

8. YVES BISSOUMA

POSITION: Midfielder

DOB: 30/08/1996

COUNTRY: Mali

'Biss' joined Albion from French club Lille in July 2018, where he had played under current Leeds boss Marcelo Bielsa. A competitive player with an eye for a spectacular goal, he made his debut against Watford in August 2018.

Following the departure of Dale Stephens to Burnley, the Mali international really came to the fore in 2020/21, earning praise for a number of eye-catching performances.

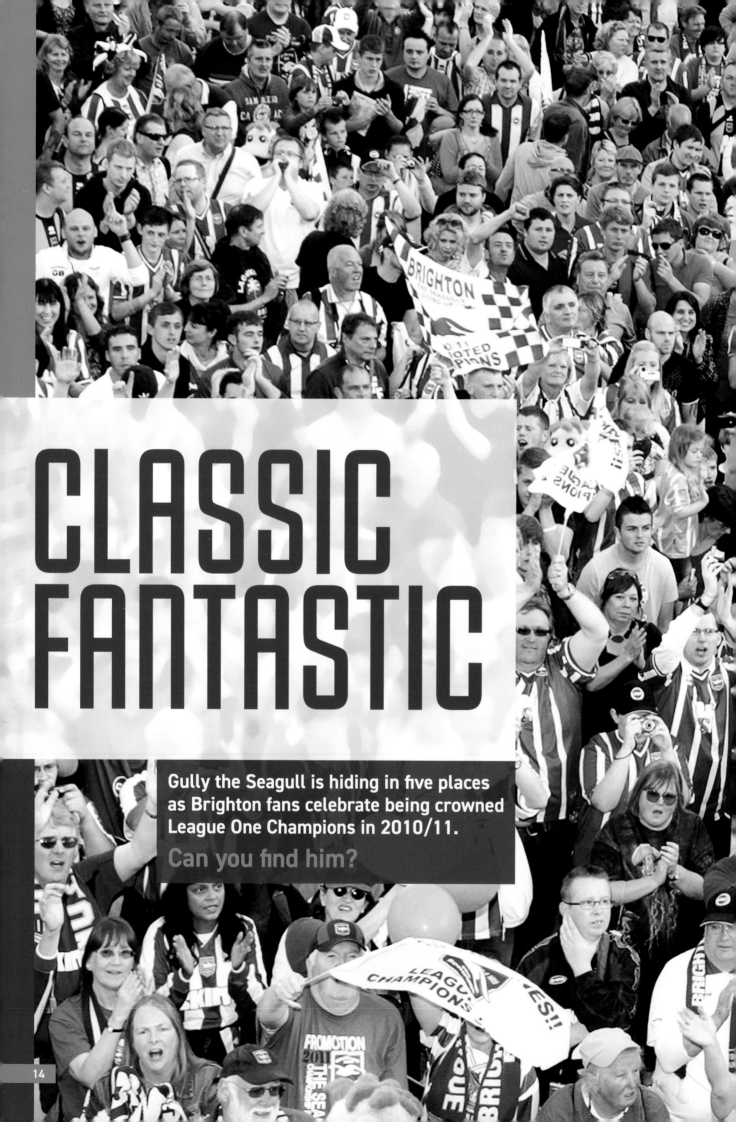

CLASSIC FANTASTIC

Gully the Seagull is hiding in five places as Brighton fans celebrate being crowned League One Champions in 2010/11.

Can you find him?

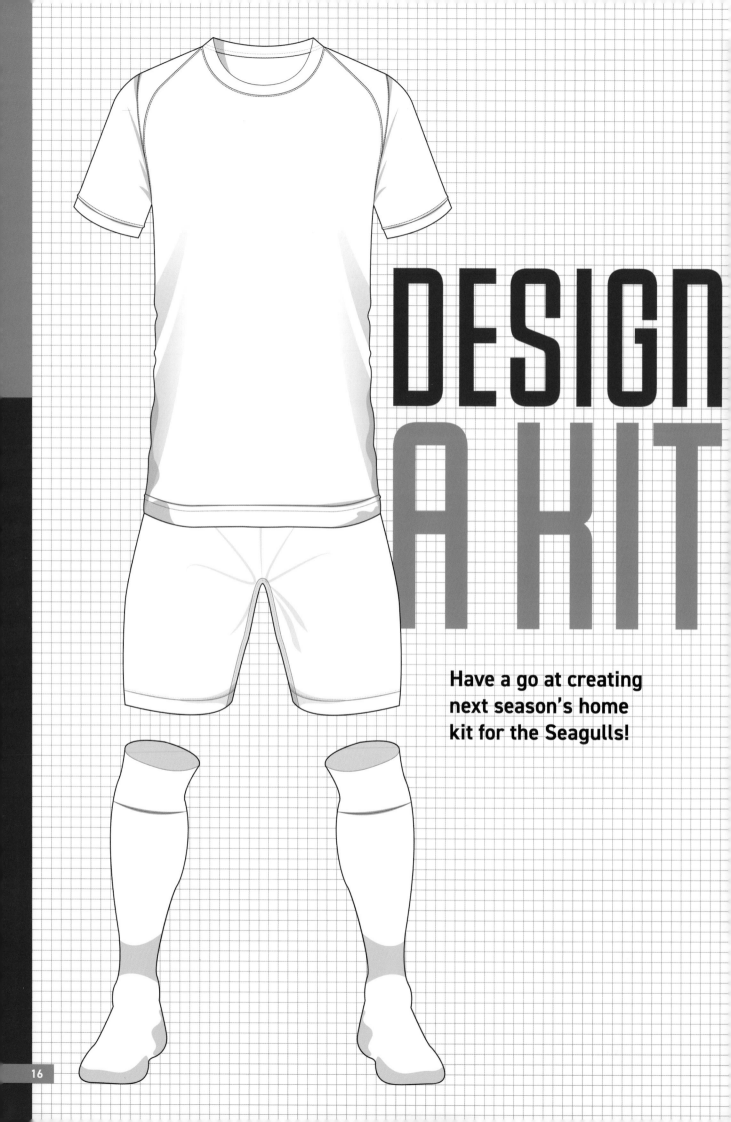

DESIGN A KIT

Have a go at creating next season's home kit for the Seagulls!

SHANE
DUFFY

The Seagulls' proud blue and white colours have been a long-held tradition at the club. However, a great deal of excitement and anticipation still surrounds the launch of every new Brighton & Hove Albion kit.

Each and every playing strip forms its own part of Albion history and supporters young and old will all have their own favourites. Let's take a look back at the first two of four of the best...

1982/83

Despite the club's long tradition of wearing blue and white striped shirts, there was a period in the early to mid 1980s when Albion's home shirt was predominately blue.

The 1982/83 season saw the first club sponsor, British Caledonian, have their company name added to the front of Albion's all-blue shirt. Produced by Adidas, this classic Albion offering was enhanced with a plain white open-necked collar and three white Adidas stripes on the side of the sleeves. The manufacturer's name and club crest sat above the sponsor's branding.

The all-blue shorts also carried the three Adidas stripes in white on the side and also the manufacturer's motif. The solid blue socks were topped with three white stripes.

DRESSED TO IMPRESS

Worn by the Albion side that plotted its way to the FA Cup Final in 1983, this particular shirt is certainly a favourite among Seagulls fans.

Despite this kit, and the yellow away version, being used throughout the unforgettable cup run, the team then had a new kit with a white v-neck collar and pinstripes produced for the FA Cup Final.

HE WORE IT WELL

Jimmy Case was a star performer in Albion's 1983 FA Cup adventure and certainly delivered the goods while wearing this famous Albion kit.

Case netted four goals in the cup run including a memorable winner against his former employers, Liverpool, in the fifth round and then found the back of the net again at the quarter-final and semi-final stages.

A true classic Brighton kit, the team's 1996/97 playing strip was manufactured by Admiral and displayed the club's traditional blue and white stripes perfectly across both the body of the shirt and the sleeves.

Club sponsor Sandtex had their logo mounted on a white background while the club crest and Admiral motif sat above. The white collar was enhanced with a two-button neck.

The all-blue shorts showed the club crest together with the manufacturer's logo. White socks were topped with a blue and red trim and also showed the Admiral motif on the shin pad area.

DRESSED TO IMPRESS

Although this kit was used through some of the club's darkest days, it was also there for some of the most important Brighton fixtures too.

This was the kit worn by Stuart Storer when he netted Albion's final goal at the Goldstone Round to secure a vital victory over Doncaster Rovers. And of course this strip signalled Albion's great escape and Football League survival at Hereford United.

HE WORE IT WELL

Surely the greatest memory Albion fans have of this kit is the sight of Robbie Reinelt scoring the all-important goal that secured the club's Football League status on the final day of the 1996/97 season.

Reinelt etched his name into Albion folklore with the equalising goal away to Hereford on 3 May 1997 that ensured the Seagulls' survival and relegation for the Bulls upon the conclusion of what was a do-or-die fixture.

1996/97

ALL KITTED OUT

9. NEAL MAUPAY

POSITION: Forward

DOB: 14/08/1996

COUNTRY: France

A prolific striker for former club Brentford in the Championship, Neal stepped up to score on his Albion debut in a Premier League win at Watford in August 2019.

The former France U21 international has been the club's leading scorer in the top flight for the past two seasons and has earned plenty of plaudits for his tireless running in the forward positions.

10. ALEXIS MAC ALLISTER

POSITION: Midfielder

DOB: 24/12/1998

COUNTRY: Argentina

Signed from Argentinos Juniors in January 2019, Alexis was loaned back to his former club for the remainder of the season, and then spent the first half of the 2019/20 season on loan at Boca Juniors.

He made his Albion debut in March 2020 against Wolves and in his breakthrough campaign of 2020/21, he netted a memorable 90th-minute equaliser at rivals Crystal Palace.

SQUAD 2021/22

11. LEANDRO TROSSARD

POSITION: Midfielder

DOB: 04/12/1994

COUNTRY: Belgium

The Belgium league's Player of the Year, having netted 14 goals in 34 appearances for champions Genk, 'Leo' joined the Albion in June 2019.

He netted on his debut against West Ham and ended the campaign with five league goals. He repeated that tally in 2020/21, including goals in the memorable home wins against Tottenham and Man City, cementing his place in Belgium's Euro 2020 squad.

12. ENOCK MWEPU

POSITION: Midfielder

DOB: 01/01/98

COUNTRY: Zambia

Albion's first signing of the summer, Enock arrived from Red Bull Salzburg on a four-year contract. He began his career with Kafue Celtic in his homeland.

He moved to Austria in the summer of 2017 and was immediately loaned out to feeder club Liefering in the Austrian First League. He then returned to establish himself in the RB first team and also made a Champions League debut against Liverpool, at Anfield, in 2019/20. A Zambia international, he has made 19 senior appearances, scoring four goals.

21

It was a successful 2020/21 season for Albion's FA WSL side as they ended the campaign in sixth place - their highest-ever top-flight finish.

It was a season of two halves for Hope Powell's side, with a 3-0 defeat at bottom-of-the-table Bristol City in January proving to be the turning point in the campaign.

After much soul-searching in the aftermath of the game, the Seagulls responded in emphatic fashion with a head-turning 2-1 defeat of table-toppers Chelsea, thanks to goals in each half from Aileen Whelan and Megan Connolly.

The incredible victory brought to an end the Blues' unbeaten WSL run that had lasted two years and some 33 games on home soil! It also gave Albion the boost they needed as the team followed up with victory against West Ham, thanks to a solitary Whelan goal, and a 2-0 win against Tottenham, following a second-half brace from Inessa Kaagman.

Whelan and Kaagman were again on target as Hope Powell's side won 2-0 at Aston Villa, making it four consecutive league wins, and while results were more chequered during the final weeks of the season, there was another stand-out result – a 1-0 win against Manchester United thanks to a Kaagman penalty.

With members of the playing staff testing positive for COVID-19 earlier in the season and fans all but absent from The People's Pension Stadium in Crawley, where Albion play their home games, sixth place was a fine achievement and Powell was certainly proud of her team.

"I am delighted with the progress we have made," she said. "I have to say that after we lost 3-0 to Bristol City at the end of January, I doubted whether we could go on and secure a top-six finish. It's been well documented that we 'reset' after that game, both the players who had some very honest conversations with each other, and us as a coaching staff.

"Going to Chelsea and beating them 2-1 in the next game gave us so much confidence but I think it was just as impressive to then go on and win the next three games as well, which took us away from the battle to avoid relegation.

"The club's stated ambition is to become a top-four WSL club in the future. There is still work to do on that but we have taken a big step forward."

ALBION WOMEN

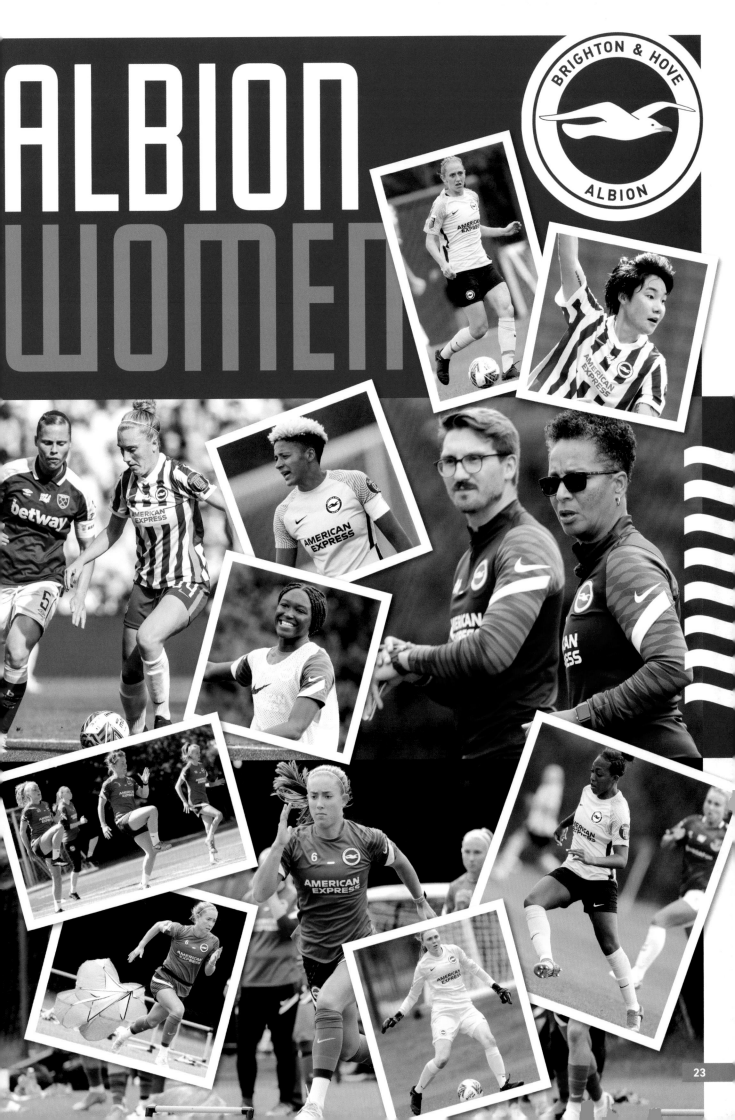

LEANDRO TROSSARD

It has been said that dribbling is a dying art. The pace of the modern game makes it more difficult, but there are players about, even in today's lightning fast conditions, who have the confidence to keep hold of the ball and take on defenders.

SOCCER SKILLS

EXERCISE ONE

As a warm-up exercise, players A and B each dribble a ball around a 20 x 10m grid, avoiding each other, but staying within the grid boundary lines.

They progress to a 'cat and mouse' race between the corners - the player with the most visits to each corner wins the race. One of the main problems in this exercise is avoiding the other player, and their ball.

EXERCISE TWO

Now for a more realistic exercise. Six players are used as shown, with three attackers and three defenders at any one time. When play starts, the players with the ball attack any of the three opposing goals, changing their target as they choose. The defenders have, simply, to stop their opposite number from scoring, but must not interfere with any other pair.

Key Factors

1. Close control.
2. Quick change of direction.
3. Acceleration away from defender.
4. Feints, to wrong-foot defender.
5. Head up to see the whole picture.

When the defenders win possession, they become the attackers, and go for goal themselves. This can be a very enjoyable practice, but also quite tiring.

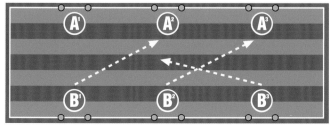

25

BRIGHTON & HOVE ALBION
1932

1
ANSWER

2
ANSWER

3
ANSWER

4
ANSWER

5
ANSWER

26

GUESS THE CLUB

6 ANSWER

7 ANSWER

8 ANSWER

9 ANSWER

10 ANSWER

Each football holds the clues to the identity of a Premier League or Football League club, how quickly can you solve them?

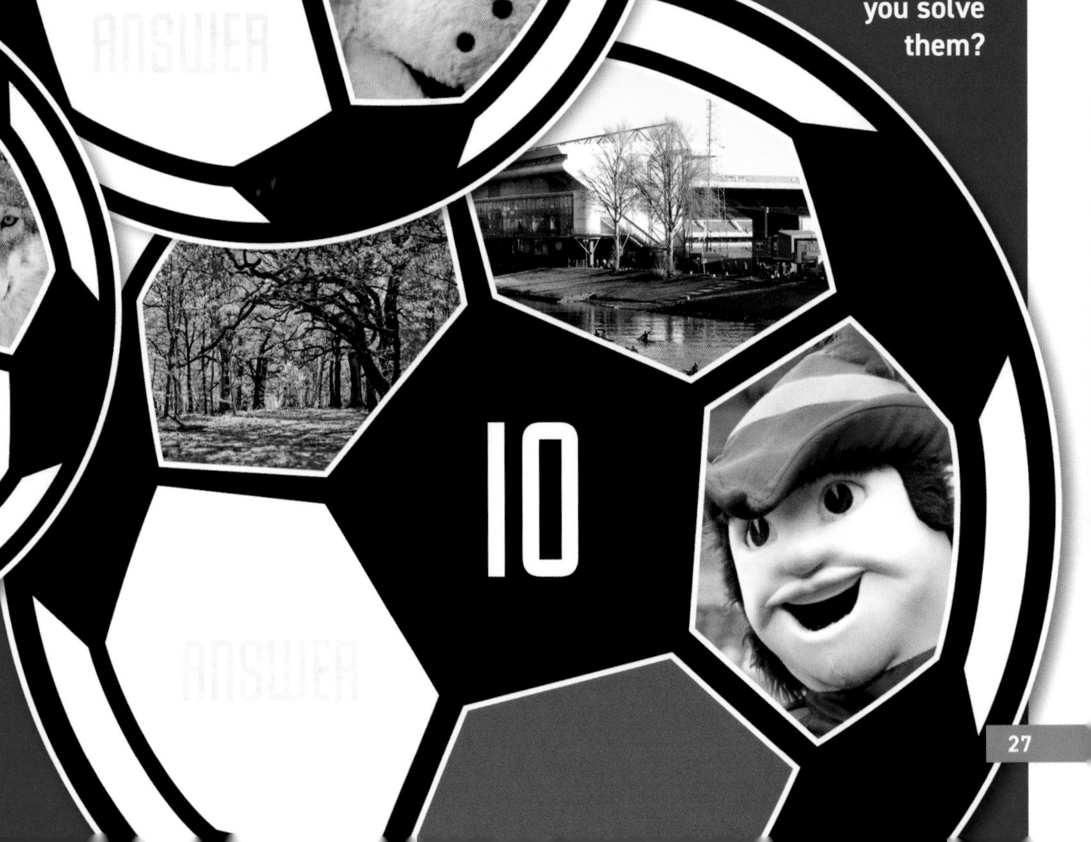

ANSWERS ON PAGE 62

BRIGHTON & HOVE ALBION

14. ADAM LALLANA

POSITION: Midfielder

DOB: 10/05/1988

COUNTRY: England

The former Southampton captain arrived at the Amex in the summer of 2020 after six successful years at Liverpool.

He came off the bench to help Albion to a famous 1-0 win at Anfield in February 2021 and scored his first goal in a 2-1 home defeat against Leicester. While he made only 16 Premier League starts, he appeared 30 times in the top flight last season.

13. PASCAL GROSS

POSITION: Midfielder

DOB: 15/06/1991

COUNTRY: Germany

A former Bundesliga player with Hoffenheim and FC Ingolstadt, Pascal joined the Seagulls ahead of the club's debut Premier League campaign.

He went on to make his 100th appearance in an EFL Cup tie at Preston in September 2020, where he was made captain. Later in the season he also skippered the side to a memorable 3-2 home win against champions Man City.

SQUAD 2021/22

15. JAKUB MODER

POSITION: Midfielder

DOB: 07/04/1999

COUNTRY: Poland

With one season of top-flight football under his belt, Moder signed from Lech Poznan in October 2020. He was loaned back to Lech but following the club's exit from the Europa League, he returned to Sussex.

Making his Albion debut in an FA Cup tie at Leicester in February 2021, he remained part of the squad and also scored for Poland against England at Wembley.

16. KJELL SCHERPEN

POSITION: Goalkeeper

DOB: 23/01/00

COUNTRY: Netherlands

A summer arrival from Ajax, Kjell started his career with hometown club Emmen, where he progressed to become a regular in the Eredivisie in 2018/19.

He joined Ajax that summer and following a prolonged spell with Jong Ajax, he made his senior debut in April 2021 following an injury to first-choice keeper Maarten Stekelenburg. The former Netherlands under-19 international made two top-flight appearances and also appeared in the Europa League against Roma before his switch to the Amex.

GOAL
OF THE SEASON

DANNY WELBECK
V LEEDS UNITED · 1 MAY 2021

A sensational Amex Stadium strike from Albion forward Danny Welbeck secured Brighton a vital three points against Leeds United in May 2021. The goal also won Welbeck the club's prestigious Goal of the Season award at the end-of-season player awards event in June.

Already a goal to the good against a Leeds side that were looking to extend an impressive six-match unbeaten run, Welbeck secured the win with 11 minutes remaining. The former England forward produced a wonderful piece of individual skill with a Cruyff-like turn to escape the attentions of Leeds defender Pascal Struijk before firing a low-angled drive past visiting 'keeper Illan Meslier.

This win gave Albion a Premier League double over the Yorkshire side and, more importantly, moved the club to within touching distance of securing top-flight football for a fifth consecutive season with four fixtures still remaining.

The goal certainly capped off a memorable afternoon's work from Welbeck who had been upended for a 14th-minute penalty from which Pascal Gross had given Albion the lead.

The skill, technique and sharp finish were always going to see Welbeck's goal as a main contender for the Goal of the Season but it had some serious competition...

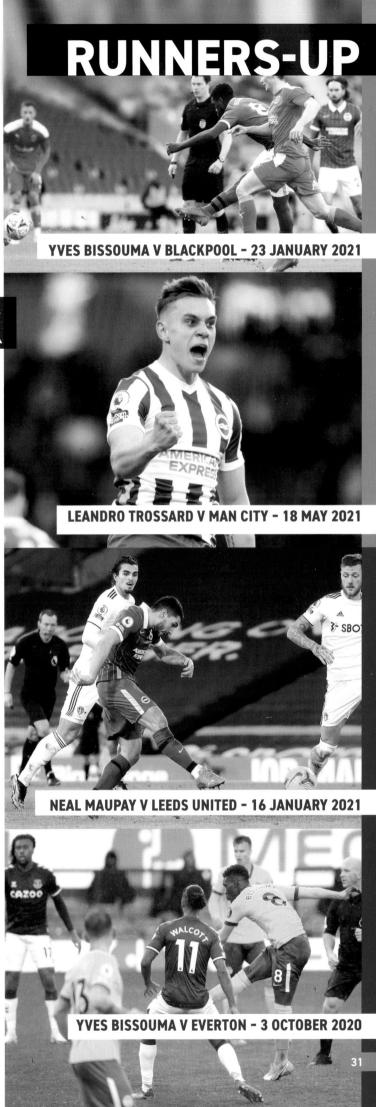

RUNNERS-UP

YVES BISSOUMA V BLACKPOOL – 23 JANUARY 2021

LEANDRO TROSSARD V MAN CITY – 18 MAY 2021

NEAL MAUPAY V LEEDS UNITED – 16 JANUARY 2021

YVES BISSOUMA V EVERTON – 3 OCTOBER 2020

Brighton-born Adam Virgo played over 150 games for the Seagulls over two separate spells with his hometown club.

He is famously remembered for his dramatic late equaliser against Swindon Town in the Second Division Play-Off semi-final in 2004. Adam was then part of the team that sealed promotion back to the Championship with a 1-0 victory over Bristol City at the Millennium Stadium.

The ultra reliable defender then further enhanced his legendary status at the club with eight goals as he helped Albion secure their Championship status in 2004/05. After a spell with Celtic he returned to Brighton in 2008.

ADAM VIRGO

SEAGULLS HEROES

TEMPERAMENT

Often faced with containing dangerous forwards, Adam Virgo had the perfect mindset for defending. He very rarely lost concentration and always kept his cool. In the heat of any on-field duel, Adam kept his mind on the task in hand and more often than not came out on top in one-on-one situations.

RALLYING CALL

Wherever he played across the back four, Virgo had the ability to lead and inspire his teammates. Always there with an encouraging call to those around him, he led by example but was never afraid to let players know if standards had dropped.

QUICK ON HIS HEELS

Adam was always alive and alert to danger and when it occurred he was quick on his heels to track and tackle opponents. Not only was he swift over the ground but he was also quick to leap and win headed duels too.

PASSING SKILLS

Always comfortable with the ball at his feet, Virgo was an accomplished ball-playing defender who could always be relied upon to bring the ball out of defence and help the side turn defence to attack.

YVES
BISSOUMA

RECORD APPEARANCE MAKER

Ernie 'Tug' Wilson holds the record for making the most appearances for Brighton & Hove Albion. However, just like record goalscorer Tommy Cook, Wilson's Brighton career began back in the 1920s.

A left-sided player, Wilson joined the club in May 1922 following a successful trial period, and as a loyal club servant he went on to amass an incredible 566 outings for Albion.

His record number of appearances is very unlikely to ever be surpassed. He also netted 71 goals in a Brighton career that spanned from 1922 to 1936. He sadly died in Hove on 27 December 1955, aged 56.

YOUNGEST PLAYER

Midfielder Jake Forster-Caskey holds the record as the youngest player to appear in a first-team match for the Albion.

Forster-Caskey is the son of former professional player Darren Caskey and the stepson of former Albion striker Nicky Forster. After progressing through the youth ranks at the club, he was handed his debut as a 76th-minute substitute on the final day of the season when an Elliott Bennett goal gave Albion a 1-0 victory over Yeovil on 8 May 2010. Forster-Caskey was aged just 16 years and 13 days old when he stepped on to the pitch at Withdean to replace Sebastien Carole.

That appearance was the first of 67 league appearances he would make for the Seagulls and saw him supersede Ian Chapman as the club's youngest player. Chapman was aged 16 years 259 days old when he debuted against Birmingham City on Valentine's Day 1987.

TOP GOALSCORER

The football landscape has certainly changed since striker Tommy Cook etched his name into Brighton & Hove Albion folklore with a club record 123 goals between 1922 and 1929.

Readers could try asking their grandparents about Cook's goalscoring prowess but chances are his achievements were even before their time of heading down to the Goldstone.

In more recent years the club has been blessed with a plethora of superb strikers, including Peter Ward, who netted a club record 32 league goals in a single season during the Seagulls' 1976/77 Third Division promotion-winning campaign. The nearest player of the modern era to get close to Cook's 123-goal haul is Glenn Murray who scored 111 goals across his two spells at the club.

RECORD MAKERS

A selection of players, games, facts and figures which all shape the club's proud history.

RECORD ATTENDANCE

As we all know, there are few better places to be than inside a packed Amex Stadium and helping cheer the Seagulls on to victory. The record attendance for a game at the Amex was set on 12 January 2019 when 30,682 fans witnessed Chris Hughton's Albion side take on title-chasing Liverpool in the Premier League.

Of course the record attendance for an Albion game was at the 1983 FA Cup Final when 100,000 spectators enjoyed the Seagulls' thrilling 2-2 draw with Manchester United at Wembley. Prior to the club's move to the Amex Stadium, their record attendance at the Goldstone Ground was set at 36,747 for a Second Division match with Fulham in December 1958. Just to complete the hat-trick of Albion ground attendances - 8,691 packed into Withdean Stadium for the League One visit of Leeds United in October 2007.

MOST INTERNATIONAL CAPS

Current Albion defender Shane Duffy holds the record as the Seagulls' most capped player. As at 1 June 2021, Duffy had won 42 caps for the Republic of Ireland despite initially playing youth and U21 football for Northern Ireland. Of his 42 caps, 37 have been won while a Brighton player albeit the most recent eight coincided with the defender's 2020/21 season-long loan at Celtic.

After 20 appearances for the Republic at U21 level, Duffy made his full international debut in a friendly match against Costa Rica in Philadelphia in June 2014. He featured for his country in the Euro 2016 finals where his heroic performance at the heart of the Republic defence helped the side to a historic victory over Italy and a place in the last 16. He captained his country for the first time in November 2019 and has retained the captaincy under new manager Stephen Kenny.

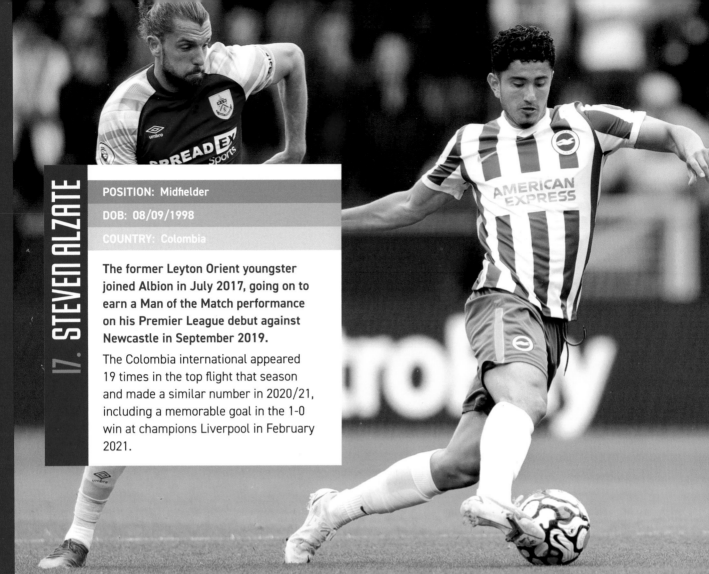

17. STEVEN ALZATE

POSITION: Midfielder

DOB: 08/09/1998

COUNTRY: Colombia

The former Leyton Orient youngster joined Albion in July 2017, going on to earn a Man of the Match performance on his Premier League debut against Newcastle in September 2019.

The Colombia international appeared 19 times in the top flight that season and made a similar number in 2020/21, including a memorable goal in the 1-0 win at champions Liverpool in February 2021.

18. DANNY WELBECK

POSITION: Forward

DOB: 26/11/1990

COUNTRY: England

The former Man United, Arsenal and Watford striker joined the Albion in October 2020 on a one-year contract and emerged as an important figure both on and off the pitch.

He netted the club's Goal of the Season, with a sublime turn and shot against Leeds United, and having impressed, he penned a new one-year contract in June.

SQUAD 2021/22

BRIGHTON & HOVE ALBION

20. SOLLY MARCH

POSITION: Midfielder

DOB: 20/07/1994

COUNTRY: England

Signed from non-league club Lewes in 2011, March has made over 200 appearances for the Seagulls and netted one of the goals which secured promotion to the Premier League, against Wigan, in April 2017.

The 2020/21 season was, arguably, his best in an Albion shirt, playing mainly as a wing-back until he sustained a knee injury in the memorable win at Liverpool which curtailed his season.

IMPOSSIBLE
Footy Decisions

Would you rather...

have to play the rest of your football games in 35 degree heat or a blizzard?

Would you rather...

have Neal Maupay's ability to score goals or Robert Sanchez's ability to save them?

Would you rather...

have a pause button or a rewind button for your life?

Would you rather...

have unlimited battery life on all your devices or free wifi wherever you go?

Would you rather...

run 100 laps of the pitch or complete 200 burpees?

Would you rather...

score the FA Cup final winning goal against your rivals in your only game for Brighton or play 300 games for the Seagulls in League One?

Would you rather...

be remembered for a terrible footy howler or be forgotten completely?

Would you rather...

sell your best player to a Premier League club for £50m or sell him abroad for £20m?

Would you rather...

have to take a penalty against Robert Sanchez or have Leandro Trossard take a penalty against you?

Would you rather...

sit right at the back during a game or have the best seats in the stadium, but not be allowed to eat, drink or use the bathroom?

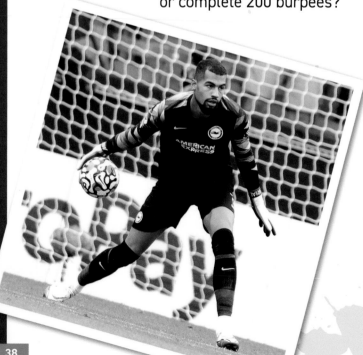

Would you rather...

be the star in League Two or a squad player in the Premier League?

Would you rather...

The Seagulls win the FA Cup or England win the World Cup?

Would you rather...

your match superstition be wearing the same socks for a season or the same underwear for a month?

Would you rather...

lose on television or win with nobody watching?

Would you rather...

have a long, average playing career or have a short, fantastic career cut short by injury?

Would you rather...

lose to your biggest rivals twice and finish top or beat them twice and finish bottom?

Would you rather...

clean the dressing room toilet with your toothbrush or the floor with your tongue?

Would you rather...

play only five minutes for BHAFC or win the Premier League with your rivals?

Would you rather...

have to wear every shirt inside out or every pair of pants backwards?

Would you rather...

give up your mobile phone for a month or bathing for a month?

Would you rather...

be alone all your life or surrounded by rival supporters?

Would you rather... play for Brighton and always lose or sit on the bench and the Seagulls always win?

Would you rather...

the half-time menu got rid of pies or pop?

Would you rather...

become a legendary manager or a legendary player?

39

ALEXIS
MAC ALLISTER

French winger Anthony Knockaert joined Brighton & Hove Albion in January 2016 from Belgian side Standard Liege.

After the disappointment of two promotion near-misses, Knockaert proved to be the real on-pitch driving force behind the Seagulls' 2016/17 promotion-winning campaign. In scintillating form throughout the season, Knockaert's 15 Championship goals and numerous assists saw him voted the EFL Championship Player of the Season.

He was also named Albion's Player of the Season at the conclusion of a memorable campaign that had seen the club return to the top flight for the first time 34 years. The 2017/18 season saw him feature in 33 Premier League games where his performances helped the Seagulls secure a 15th place finish among English football's elite.

ANTHONY KNOCKAERT

SEAGULLS HEROES

INTELLIGENCE

A player's football intelligence is often spoken about and Anthony Knockaert had it in abundance. He had the skill of making time on the ball, orchestrating the pattern of play and playing creative forward balls. He also had that ability of knowing the runs a teammate would make and the ability to find them with the minimum of fuss.

SHOOTING

Despite the majority of his Albion goals coming from his preferred left boot, Anthony appeared equally as comfortable on his right foot and was never afraid to use his perceived weaker foot to shoot or cross.

EYE FOR AN OPENING

Not only was Knockaert extremely comfortable on the ball but he also showed great vision and awareness on the pitch. He appeared to have the perfect eye for a quick pass to help the Seagulls mount attacking moves.

QUICK FEET

Naturally blessed with exceptional close control and dribbling skills, Anthony Knockaert had the ability to jinx his way past opponents and into dangerous areas. Always indentified as the dangerman, Anthony often proved to be a tricky player for the opposition to get to grips with.

2010/11

Albion maintained their long-standing relationship with Italian kit manufacturer Errea who produced a simple but smart playing strip for the final season at Withdean.

The kit had thin white strips down the body of the shirt and the sleeves. The v-neck collar was also blue with a white trim. The club crest sat opposite the manufacturer's logo with the club sponsor's branding sitting below.

The solid blue shorts had white piping at the base and carried the Errea logo and club crest while the blue socks had a white top and Errea branding on the shin pad area.

DRESSED TO IMPRESS

Albion signed off from Withdean in style in 2010/11 – not only did they look the part in their excellent playing strip but the team turned on the style with their performances too as they were crowned League One champions.

The Seagulls held off the challenge of south coast rivals Southampton to land the title with a 95-point haul and ensure that when the club moved to the Amex Stadium in 2011/12 their new home would he hosting Championship football.

HE WORE IT WELL

A top-quality performer during his two seasons at Withdean, attacking midfielder Elliott Bennett was a key member of the team's 2010/11 title-winning campaign.

Bennett chipped in with six League One goals and his positive play created a host of opportunities for others. His form in 2010/11 secured him a summer transfer to the Premier League when he joined Norwich City.

The Seagulls' kit was produced by Nike for a fourth consecutive season as the team tackled life in the Premier League for the first time in 2017/18.

A few tweaks were made to the previous season's offering and included an all-blue shoulder and sleeve offering with the traditional blue and white stripes making up the front body of the shirt. A small section of yellow was added to the v-neck collar with the Nike swoosh, club crest and club sponsor all on the front of the shirt.

The blue shorts had a thin white panel on each side and carried the club crest and manufacturer's logo. The all-white socks had the Nike swoosh on the front in blue.

DRESSED TO IMPRESS

Having won promotion from the Championship the previous season, Albion managed to maintain their Premier League status with two games to spare after recording a memorable victory over Manchester United in their final home fixture.

Under the management of Chris Hughton, Albion ended the 2017/18 season in 15th place after hitting the magic 40-point mark.

HE WORE IT WELL

Often decked in his all-orange goalkeeping kit, Australian stopper Mat Ryan enjoyed an impressive debut season.

A confident, agile and well-built 'keeper, Ryan was ever-present in 2017/18 and pulled off a number of match-winning saves for the Seagulls to help maintain the club's Premier League status.

2017/18

ALL KITTED OUT

23. JASON STEELE

POSITION: Goalkeeper

DOB: 18/08/1990

COUNTRY: England

The experienced former Middlesbrough, Blackburn and Sunderland 'keeper signed for the Seagulls in June 2018. While he hadn't made a Premier League appearance in his first three seasons, he made four appearances in cup competitions in 2020/21.

He also emerged as the preferred back-up to first-choice keeper Robert Sanchez, earning a new contract with the club.

24. SHANE DUFFY

POSITION: Defender

DOB: 01/01/92

COUNTRY: The Republic of Ireland

The former Everton youngster made his professional debut for the Toffees against AEK Athens in the Europa League in December 2009.

Loan spells at Burnley, Scunthorpe and Yeovil followed before a move to Blackburn in 2014. After two years with Rovers, he made the switch to the Albion and went on to play a key role in the Seagulls' promotion to the Premier League and was voted the club's Player of the Season in the top flight in 2018/19. The Republic of Ireland international spent last season on loan at Celtic.

SQUAD 2021/22

28. HAYDON ROBERTS

POSITION: Defender

DOB: 10/05/02

COUNTRY: England

The homegrown centre-back came through the club's academy to make his senior debut at home to Aston Villa in the EFL Cup in September 2019.

He capped a fine performance with a goal in the 3-1 defeat. Within weeks of his second appearance against Portsmouth the following season, he made a season-long loan move to League One Rochdale.

An England U18 international, he returned to Sussex in the summer, and this season has been elevated to the Albion first-team squad, making his first appearance of the season against Cardiff City in the EFL Cup.

BRIGHTON & HOVE ALBION

NEAL MAUPAY

One of a player's greatest assets is the ability to win the ball. The following exercise can be used to improve a player's tackling abilities.

TACKLING

SOCCER SKILLS

EXERCISE

Set up a 10m x 20m grid.

In this two-on-two exercise, the aim of the game is to score a goal by taking the ball past the two opposing defenders, to the end line, and stand on the ball. The defenders just have to stop them.

As well as producing plenty of opportunities for the defenders to tackle, this session will test the defenders' abilities to work together, and communicate.

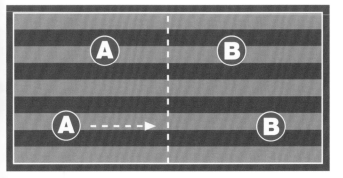

Key Factors

1. **Be patient - do not dive in.**

2. **Stay on your feet if possible.**

3. **Time the tackle with bodyweight behind it.**

4. **Be determined to win it.**

The reason that great players win so many tackles is not just because they know how to tackle and have good technique, it is because they have big hearts and are determined to win their challenges on the pitch.

ODDBALLS

Three of the four pictures in each football represent a Premier League or Football League club, can you figure out the football club as well as the odd one out?

1

A
B
C
D

ANSWER

2

A
B
C
D

1898

ANSWER

3

A
B
C
D

ANSWER

4

A
B
C
D

FOOTBALL CLUB

ANSWER

5

A
B
C
D

ANSWER

48

ANSWERS ON PAGE 62

6

B A C D

BRIGHTON & HOVE ALBION

1905

7

B A C D

ANSWER

8

B A C D

ANSWER

10

B A C D

ANSWER

9

A B C D

ANSWER

FOOTBALL CLUB

PLAYERS'
PLAYER OF THE SEASON

LEWIS DUNK

The ultimate seal of approval on a player's contribution to a season is when his achievements are acknowledged by his fellow teammates. Therefore, securing the prestigious Players' Player of the Season award really is a key honour when the Brighton & Hove Albion end-of-season awards are handed out.

The winner of the award for 2020/21 was inspirational skipper Lewis Dunk. The Brighton-born defender is almost seen as the supporter on the pitch by the fans, but the 29-year-old centre-back is equally respected by his Albion teammates.

The home-grown hero, who has been at the heart of the club's successful era at the Amex Stadium, made 33 Premier League appearances last season and chipped in with five goals as the Seagulls maintained their top-flight status for a fifth consecutive season.

Dunk's form throughout the campaign, particularly in the second half of the season, was immense and he played a key role in the club pulling away from the threat of danger. His club form was reminiscent of the consistency he showed to earn his first England cap v USA in 2018.

A reliable and fully committed defender, Dunk also made his presence felt at the attacking end of the pitch too as he contributed vital goals to the Seagulls' season. The skipper enjoyed a real purple patch over the festive period – on target in the 2-2 draw at West Ham, he was also on hand to net Brighton's third goal against Wolves at the Amex to secure a vital point in a thrilling 3-3 draw.

However, the most important of his five goals came on 14 March when he opened the scoring in Albion's vital 2-1 win away to south cost rivals Southampton.

Having agreed a new five-year contract in August 2020 ahead of the 2020/21 season, securing the Player' Player of the Season award really was the icing on the cake following yet another impressive and important contribution to the Albion cause from Lewis Dunk.

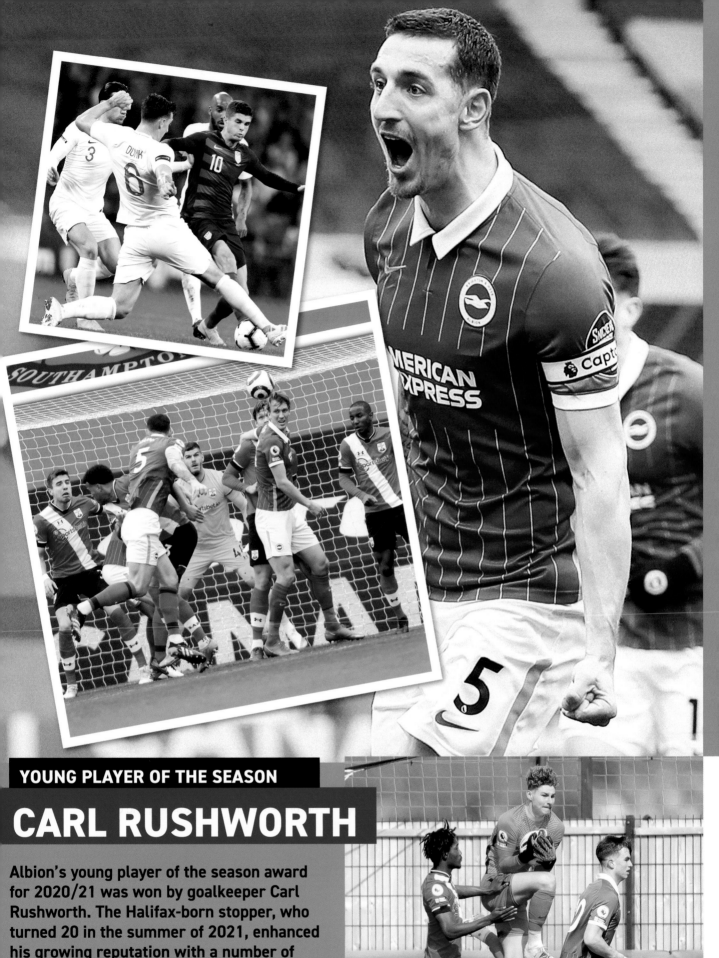

CARL RUSHWORTH

Albion's young player of the season award for 2020/21 was won by goalkeeper Carl Rushworth. The Halifax-born stopper, who turned 20 in the summer of 2021, enhanced his growing reputation with a number of impressive performances for the club's under-23 side.

Seeing the success that Robert Sanchez has enjoyed with the Albion first team, Rushworth will no doubt look to follow suit and he has been sent out on loan to Walsall to gain first-team experience this season.

ADAM
LALLANA

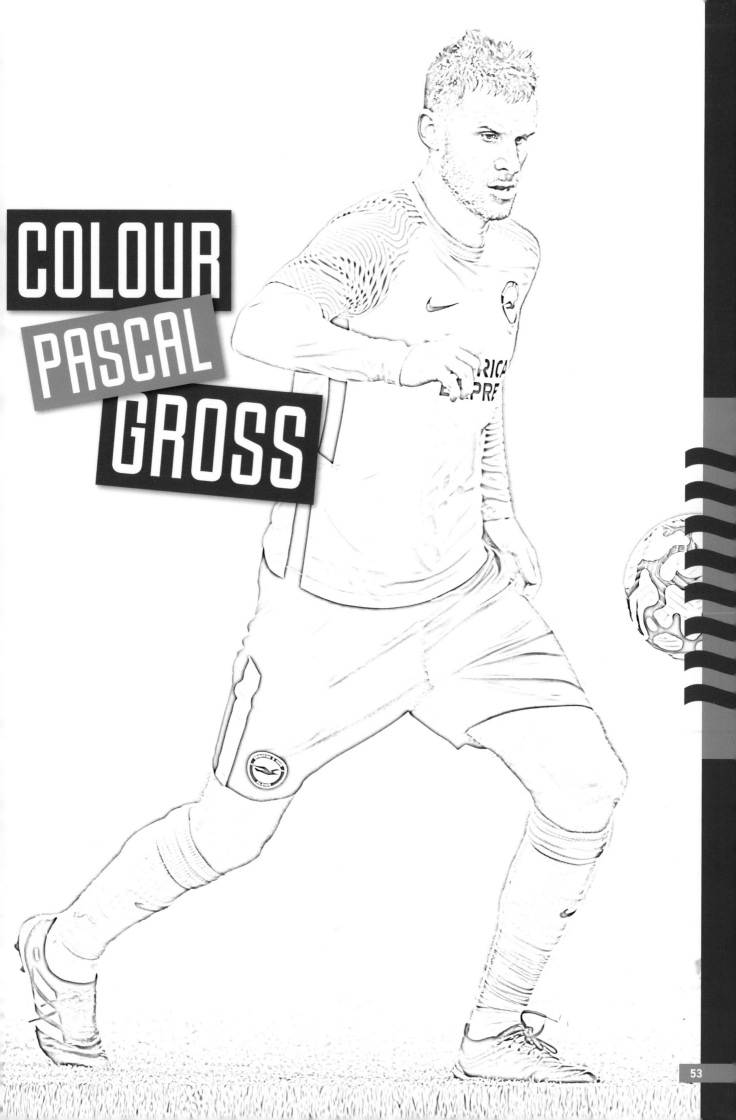

COLOUR
PASCAL
GROSS

SQUAD 2021/22

30. TAYLOR RICHARDS

POSITION: Midfielder

DOB: 04/12/2000

COUNTRY: England

Taylor Richards joined Albion in July 2019 from Manchester City, before signing a new three-year contract with the club in August 2021.

Taylor broke into City's U23s during the 2018/19 Premier League 2 campaign, and ended the season with an impressive 10 goals from 29 appearances. He spent 2020/21 on loan with Doncaster Rovers, where he scored 11 goals in 48 outings.

He went onto make his Premier League debut for Albion at the beginning of the 2021/22 campaign, in a 2-0 home defeat to Everton.

33. DAN BURN

POSITION: Defender

DOB: 09/05/1992

COUNTRY: England

The left-sided defender has played in every division from the National League upwards with Darlington, Fulham, Wigan and the Albion.

He joined Brighton in the summer of 2018, after winning League One with the Latics, and has since made over 60 Premier League appearances.

In May 2021 he scored his first goal for the club in the 3-2 home win over Manchester City.

34. JOEL VELTMAN

POSITION: Defender

DOB: 15/01/1992

COUNTRY: Netherlands

With three Eredivisie titles to his name, Joel moved from Ajax to Brighton in July 2020.

He was a versatile performer for the Dutch giants and has also played in various defensive and midfield roles for the Seagulls - most notably at right wing-back following the long-term injury sustained by Tariq Lamptey. Joel's form earned him a place in the Netherlands' squad for Euro 2020.

BRIGHTON & HOVE ALBION

1. WHO AM I?

I was born in Bath in 1989

I began my pro career with Plymouth Argyle

I was initially on loan at Brighton before joining permanently

I scored 20 goals in the club's 2010/11 promotion-winning season

I am currently playing for a Premier League rival

3. WHO AM I?

I joined the Seagulls in 2008

I was signed from Rochdale

I marked my home debut for Albion with two goals against Crewe Alexandra

I left Brighton in 2011 but returned to the club in 2016

Across my two spells with Brighton I have scored 111 goals for the club

GUESS WHO

2. WHO AM I?

I was born in Preston in 1957

I joined Brighton in 1977

I made my Albion debut in a south coast derby match against Southampton

I later played international football for the Republic of Ireland

I spent many seasons on television as a Match of the Day pundit

As a youngster I was
on the books at Chelsea

I began my professional
career with Gillingham

I enjoyed two
separate spells
as a Brighton player

I played Premier
League football with
Norwich City

Since hanging up my
boots I have joined the
Seagulls' coaching staff

4. WHO AM I?

I joined the Seagulls in 1983

I was signed from
Nottingham Forest

I played football for nine
clubs but made more league
appearances for Albion than
any other club I represented

I scored 16 goals from
midfield for Brighton in
the 1985/86 season

I won 24 caps for Northern
Ireland before embarking on
a lengthy managerial career

5. WHO AM I?

6. WHO AM I?

I was born in Spain in 1980

I joined Albion
from Valencia in 2012

I scored my first goal
for the Seagulls against
Bolton Wanderers

In seven years as a
Brighton player I made 235
appearances for the club

I made my last appearance
for Albion on the final day
of the 2018/19 season

ANSWERS ON PAGE 62

Goalscoring legend Bobby Zamora enjoyed two spells with the club and his £100,000 arrival from Bristol Rovers in 2000 remains one of the club's best pieces of transfer business.

During his first full season he netted an incredible 31 goals in all competitions as Brighton won the Third Division title in 2000/01. His 32 goals the following season proved to be the vital ingredient as Albion achieved back-to-back promotions when they landed the 2001/02 Second Division title.

After leaving the Seagulls in 2003 for Premier League Tottenham Hotspur, Zamora made an emotional return to Brighton for the 2015/16 campaign and helped Albion reach the Championship Play-Offs.

SEAGULLS HEROES

HEADERS

A number of Bobby Zamora's 90 Albion goals came from headers. A real threat in the air as well as on the deck, Bobby had the power to out-jump defenders and then use his head to direct the ball past the 'keeper and into the opposition's net.

ENCOURAGEMENT

Often employed as the focal point of the attack, Bobby could be relied upon to advise and encourage teammates to play the ball into areas where he could be most effective and cause danger to the opposition.

CHEST CONTROL

As a robust and powerful centre-forward who led the Seagulls' attack so well, Zamora was blessed with a great ability to play with his back to goal and take the ball under control on his chest. He could then hold up play while others arrived in support or lay the ball off to a teammate.

GOALS

The majority of Bobby's goals for Brighton came from his trusty right foot. With the ability to take shots first-time, even if under pressure from a defender, when Zamora pulled the trigger with his right foot it rarely let him down.

ADAM WEBSTER

FAST FORWARD >>

Here are Gully's predictions for 2021/22. Do you agree?...

PREMIER LEAGUE TOP SCORER

Harry Kane

PREMIER LEAGUE WINNERS

Manchester United

PREMIER LEAGUE RUNNERS-UP

Chelsea

FA CUP WINNERS

Brighton & Hove Albion

FA CUP RUNNERS-UP

Leeds United

LEAGUE CUP WINNERS

Arsenal

LEAGUE CUP RUNNERS-UP

Leicester City

CHAMPIONSHIP WINNERS
Fulham

CHAMPIONSHIP RUNNERS-UP
Derby County

CHAMPIONSHIP PLAY-OFF WINNERS
Reading

CHAMPIONSHIP TOP SCORER
Ivan Cavaleiro

SEAGULLS TOP SCORER
Neal Maupay

CHAMPIONS LEAGUE WINNERS
Barcelona

CHAMPIONS LEAGUE RUNNERS-UP
Real Madrid

SEAGULLS PLAYER OF THE YEAR
Lewis Dunk

EUROPA LEAGUE WINNERS
West Ham United

EUROPA LEAGUE RUNNERS-UP
Lazio

ANSWERS

PAGE 11
SOCCER SEARCH

Bicycle Kick.

PAGE 14
CLASSIC FANTASTIC

PAGE 26
GUESS THE CLUB

1. Newcastle United. 2. Wigan Athletic. 3. Leeds United.
4. Charlton Athletic. 5. Coventry City. 6. AFC Wimbledon.
7. Liverpool. 8. Millwall. 9. Wolverhampton Wanderers.
10. Nottingham Forest.

PAGE 48
ODD BALLS

1. Sunderland, C. 2. Portsmouth, C. 3. Arsenal, B.
4. Crewe Alexandra, A. 5. Queens Park Rangers, C.
6. Crystal Palace, B. 7. Tottenham Hotspur, B.
8. Reading, B. 9. Birmingham City, C.
10. West Ham United, D.

PAGE 56
GUESS WHO?

1. Ashley Barnes. 2. Mark Lawrenson. 3. Glenn Murray.
4. Andrew Crofts. 5. Danny Wilson. 6. Bruno.